Winning at Slot Machines

Winning at
Slot Machines

by JIM REGAN

A CITADEL PRESS BOOK
Published by Carol Publishing Group

Carol Publishing Group Edition - 1994

A Citadel Press Book
Published by Carol Publishing Group
Citadel Press is a registered trademark of Carol Communications, Inc.

Editorial Offices: 600 Madison Avenue, New York, NY 10022
Sales & Distribution Offices: 120 Enterprise Avenue, Secaucus, NJ 07094
In Canada: Canadian Manda Group, P.O. Box 920, Station U, Toronto,
Ontario, M8Z 5P9, Canada

Queries regarding rights and permissions should be addressed to:
Carol Publishing Group, 600 Madison Avenue, New York, NY 10022

Manufactured in the United States of America
ISBN 0-8065-0973-2

20 19 18 17 16 15 14 13 12 11 10

Carol Publishing Group books are available at special discounts
for bulk purchases, sales promotions, fund raising, or
educational purposes. Special editions can also be created to
specifications. For details contact: Special Sales Department,
Carol Publishing Group, 120 Enterprise Ave., Secaucus, NJ 07094

ACKNOWLEDGMENTS

The author wishes to acknowledge the assistance of Jean Stoess, a Reno freelance writer/editor, who edited and typed the manuscript of this book.

He also wishes to thank Advanced Graphics of Reno for the slot machine award glass illustrations.

Contents

Winning at Slot Machines

CHAPTER 1

Introduction: Playing Smart

More and more people in this country and around the world are willing to "take a chance on chance" these days. In other words, the public seems to be looking more and more favorably at gaming. The growing popularity of lotteries and the fact that many states are taking another look at various other forms of legalized gambling substantiates the claim that public attitudes toward games of chance are changing. The success of casinos in New Jersey, for example, could well be viewed as proof of a growing interest in this leisure-time activity.

No other gaming device has caught the attention of the growing number of casino gaming customers as has the new generation of slot machines. Slots are not what they used to be, and some of the giant "progressives" these days offer jackpots that never existed in the past. It isn't unusual to read in a newspaper now about someone hitting a progressive slot machine for a million dollars or more. Once the babysitter for the wives of the "real players," slots have come into their own.

Slot machines of various kinds can be found in many states and foreign countries, and the number is growing all the time. In Nevada, for example, the Economic Research Division of the Nevada Gaming Control Board reported that the total number of slot machines statewide skyrocketed from 36,890 in 1971 to 94,684 at June 30, 1984. Slot machines alone produce more than half of Nevada's gaming revenues.

Unfortunately, like just about everything else in this world, slot machines are not as simple as they once were. You really need to know what you are doing if you sincerely want to win. What you don't know about playing today's slots can cost you plenty.

In the pages ahead, you will learn about the types of slot machines and how they actually pay off. You will also learn about gaming laws, the IRS and you, and general rules of gaming conduct. In addition, we will explore some of the myths about slot play. A few years ago, these and many of the other subjects in this book were not very important to most slot machine players. Today, however, in order to have any realistic hope of doing well at slots, you should know all the information you can get.

If you're a serious slot player, you need to identify your objective in choosing the slots before beginning to play. Is it to win big bucks, perhaps a quarter million or more? To win one hundred to one thousand times over the actual amount of the wager? Just to double or triple the total amount played? To get the longest possible playing time on the least amount of money? Or just for the fun and amusement?

In order to be able to play smart, you must match the objective with the right kind of slots—and that is no easy task for the uninformed. So before you play a slot machine again, unless you have money to throw away, read every word on the following pages.

CHAPTER 2

Myths and Schemes of Slot Play

The myths about playing slot machines are almost endless. For example, there are myths about when to play, myths about how to spot good machines, and myths about knowing which are the "house" games. Let's examine some of these mistaken ideas and some of the other misleading information we have all heard about.

"Where Are the Loose Machines?"

Do casinos really have "loose slots"? According to this myth, and because the term loose slots is so familiar, the answer would seem to be yes. Even casinos themselves advertise that they have the "loosest slots in town." So, how do you find these loose machines?

Well, not only are there myths about the location of loose machines, there are also tales about the best time of

15

the day or the best day of the week to find one. Do any of these sound familiar?

—The machines on the aisles (or near the windows) pay off better because other people can see you win and then will want to play, too.
—Don't play slots during the daytime; they tighten the machines then so it will look like people are winning more often at night.
—Only play slots on Fridays or Saturdays because by then they've made their money for the week and will be less stingy.

The strangest myth of all is:

—Put your hand on the front of the machine; if it feels warmer than the other machines, it's a loose one.

Actually, there are hundreds of false ideas about finding loose slots and winning tons of dough.

But, first of all, let's consider what is meant by the term *loose slots*. Does it mean that the parts inside one machine are literally looser than in some other machines? Does it imply that if a machine is more tightly bolted together it will be less generous? Many people actually believe that this is true, so they seek out only those machines that make a loud noise when played. These players look for the older mechanical machines that may clang and rattle when the handle is pulled and the reels are spinning. These people are sure they've found the secret of how to play slots.

Other players use the term loose in the figurative sense of the word, believing that how often or how much the slot machine pays off, rather than the way it looks or sounds, is what makes a machine loose. Again, the advertising of many casinos would seem to support this definition of loose slots because it implies that the casino is willing to lose money on some machines in order to attract business. Such familiar statements as "We Have More Slot Winners" or "Our Slots Pay More Jackpots" are designed to make prospective players think they will win more at that casino. The implication here is that the less money the casino makes on slots, the luckier the slot players will be.

But this is not necessarily so. The terms loose and tight are only relative, and have very little influence on whether the individual player wins or loses. Some machines (called *high-frequency machines*) are set to pay out fewer coins more frequently, and other machines pay out more coins less often. The end result is about the same, even though many players believe that the machines that pay more often are the looser ones.

Let's clear up another myth of so-called loose slot machines. Many people believe that inside every slot machine is a dial or a level or special wires or a switch that will make the machine pay off or—if you are winning—not pay off. I've overheard hundreds of slot players say to a casino employee in all seriousness, "While you're at it, make it win for me." Please be advised, dear reader, that there are no magic buttons or secret switches that will make your slot machine looser or tighter. Casinos do not go around at four A.M. and tighten all the machines until the next evening or the next weekend.

To start with, it would be far too expensive and time-consuming to attempt to increase or decrease the payout percentage on most regular slot machines. Except for certain electronic machines and video slots, *index discs* and *reel strips* would have to be changed, as would, in many cases, the payout schedule glass on the front of the machine. It could take hours just to change one slot. More importantly, state gaming regulations require that each slot machine's payout percentage be recorded and maintained by the casino, and any changes must be officially reported.

I don't want you to get the idea that the slot machines in all casinos are exactly the same, because they are not. But I will tell you that they are all competitive. In some casinos there may be a greater number of high-frequency machines; other casinos may have machines with larger jackpots; and still other casinos may offer machines with special bonuses. But it is a waste of time to look for or hope to find slot machines on which a casino deliberately expects to lose money.

"If You Know How to Pull the Handle the Right Way, You Can Get the Machine to Pay Off More Often"

Some people pull the handle ever so slowly, a quarter-inch at a time, believing the slower they pull, the slower the reels will spin around (or something), and that will help them to win. Other people do just the opposite. The faster or harder they can pull the handle, the better. When a casino employee expresses concern for the welfare of the machine after such treatment, these players are all the more convinced that they have found the secret to success for playing slots—otherwise, the casino wouldn't care if they tore off the machine handles!

There are also variations of the slow and fast pulling

of slot handles. One person likes to pull the handle down slowly and force it back up abruptly. Another player will yank the handle down and hold it down until the reels index (stop spinning). And so on. None of these techniques have anything to do with how a machine will pay or how often you can win.

Let me add a word of warning, however. Once in a great while you will discover a machine on which you can pull the handle and make the reels spin without putting in any money. First of all, chances are good that this free-playing machine will not pay when you hit something. But even if it does, you would be well advised to stop playing this machine immediately and call an attendant. Why? It is against the law in most areas to knowingly play a malfunctioning slot machine. You will not be allowed to keep any money you received from the machine, and you will not be paid for any jackpot you might hit. In addition, chances are good that another customer would see you free-playing this machine and report it to the casino, which could result in a lot of embarrassment—or worse. Use good judgment.

"Dollar Slot Machines Pay Off Better Than Nickel, Dime, or Quarter Machines"

This popular notion suggests that because you aren't playing dollars, the smaller denomination machines will penalize you in some way. In other words, you get a better deal if you can play the dollar machines. Well, folks, it ain't exactly so. It is entirely possible to find three identical machines in the same casino: one a nickel, one a quarter, and one a dollar. Except for the size of the coin each machine will accept, they are exactly alike—and you can be just as lucky playing nickels as dollars. In fact, I'm sure you could find some nickel machines that offer a greater payback than some dollar machines.

So, to say your chances of winning are not as good unless you are playing dollar slots isn't quite correct. This shouldn't cause you to conclude, however, that there are no differences between dollar machines as a whole and their smaller-denomination cousins. Dollar machines tend to have a smaller *hold*, in general, than do the other machines. Hold is what the machine keeps for the casino. (Later in this book, you will learn that several factors determine how slots pay off; the hold is only one of these factors.)

It is important to remember that you could be just as lucky playing nickels, dimes, or quarters as you could play-ing dollars. And if you aren't winning, at least you know your money may last a little longer.

"This Machine Has Been Played for Hours and Hasn't Paid a Jackpot, So It's About Ready to Hit"

Maybe, and maybe not! Viewed in one way, there is an element of truth to this myth because the longer the machine is played, the greater the probability that it will hit a jackpot. It is for this reason that people are willing to keep dropping coins into a cold machine, with the result that many expectant slot players become disappointed losers. By the time a jackpot finally hits, the player may very well have gone broke or put more money into the machine than the jackpot will pay out. The casino is the winner in either case.

As will be discussed in the next chapter, slots operate

randomly. There is no little counter or clock inside that signals when it is time to pay out a jackpot.

One of the common "secrets" found in books that claim to teach readers "how to win at slots" is to ask a changeperson or other slot employee to point out a machine that hasn't hit for a while or is, in the employee's opinion, due to hit. Although discouraged by management from recommending machines to players, employees often will do so anyway. This is because they know that a player who then hits a jackpot is very likely to tip the employee who recommended that machine. No jackpot, no tip, of course, but employees have nothing to lose by recommending a machine, even when they have no idea when it last paid a jackpot. So, slot employee advice is not a sure thing, but such information, when applied to what you will learn in the pages ahead, may be helpful to deciding when and where to play.

Just remember, waiting out a jackpot can be dangerous to your pocketbook, so don't ever invest more than you can possibly win on any one machine.

There are many more miscellaneous notions and meaningless schemes that claim to provide a fool-proof system for winning at slots. But the only way to improve your chances is to understand how slot machines differ one from another and how to choose a machine that is most compatible with your wagering objectives.

If there were a fool-proof way to beat slot machines that was known only to the people who work in casinos, how many casino workers do you think would be willing to labor away each and every day for an hourly wage? The truth is, there is no secret get-rich-quick scheme for playing slots. There are only sensible and logical ways to maximize your chances of being lucky without blindly losing your hard-earned money to the "one-armed bandit."

CHAPTER 3

Theoretical Odds: How Slots Pay Off

"Around and around she goes, and where she stops nobody knows." That's not good enough? You need a more complete explanation? OK, here goes. But if you get lost, please remember that you can always refer back to this first sentence and be done with it.

Slot machines operate on the basis of random selection and theoretical odds. *Random selection* means that no single outcome can be predicted at any given time. In other words, ". . . where she stops nobody knows." *Theoretical odds* indicates that over an extended period of time, results of the random outcomes can be predicted.

Let's begin by talking about an actual slot machine. For the sake of this discussion, we will select a common three-reel machine with symbols of fruit, bars, and 7s on each reel. Starting with the first reel on the left, we count a total of 22 symbols on each of the three reels. Because there are no blank spaces on these reels, 1 of the 22 symbols on each reel will stop on the payline of the machine each time the machine is played. So, it would be correct to say that each reel can stop in any one of 22 places. In slot machine talk we would say that each reel has 22 *stops*. Therefore, the machine in our example is a 22-stop machine. Conventional reel-type slots will usually be 20-, 22-, or 25-stop machines.

Now, then, if each reel has only one jackpot symbol, a 7, and three 7s must line up in order to win, can we figure out how often this machine will hit a jackpot? The answer is yes—at least theoretically. We would begin by finding out the total number of different positions in which the three reels can possibly stop without stopping in the combination twice. This is called finding the machine's *cycle*. Because we already know each reel can stop in any of 22 places and because there are three reels, it's a simple matter of multiplying $22 \times 22 \times 22$. This figures out to 10,648.

Now we know there are 10,648 separate places the three reels can stop, but what's the possibility of lining up the three 7s? Because there is only one 7 per reel, mathematically it looks like this: $1 \times 1 \times 1$, which, of course, equals 1. Therefore, only once out of more than 10,600 reel spins is it likely that the jackpot will be hit.

But, remember that we are only speaking theoretically. We are not saying that the person who pulls the handle of this slot machine every 10,648 times will hit the jackpot. And while this particular machine we are discussing has just one 7 on each reel, don't assume there is only one jackpot symbol per reel on every slot machine in the world. On the other hand, there need not be more than one jackpot symbol

Sample Reel Strips for 22-Stop Slot Machine

Cherry	Oranqe	Plum
Plum	Bell	Bell
Bell	Bar	Orange
Bar	Cherry	Plum
Bell	Bar	Orange
Orange	Cherry	Cherry
Bell	Bar	Plum
Plum	Bar	Orange
Bell	Orange	Plum
Bell	Bar	Orange
Cherry	Cherry	Plum
Plum	Bar	Plum
Bell	Plum	Orange
Bar	Bar	Cherry
Bell	Orange	Plum
Orange	Cherry	Plum
Bell	Bar	Orange
Plum	Bar	Plum
Bell	Bell	Bar
Bell	Bar	Plum
Plum	Cherry	Orange
7	7	7

per reel on any given slot machine—and many machines are just this way.

Occasionally, slot players become convinced that their machine does not have a jackpot symbol on every reel. Sometimes they even request that the machine be opened so they can examine the reel in question. Rest assured that there has to be at least one jackpot symbol on each reel— or the casino or store operator will be out of business and in big legal trouble.

The odds of 1 in 10,648 that each of the three reels will stop on a 7 are only theoretical because of the element of random selection. It is because of this entirely random outcome each time the handle is pulled that it is possible to win two or more jackpots on the same machine in a relatively short period of time. Although unlikely, hitting jackpots back-to-back does happen occasionally.

Each pay combination on any machine can be computed in the same manner as we just did with the 7s. This time let's look for cherries on each of the three reels of our sample machine. On reel number one (the reel on the left as we face the machine), we count a total of two cherries; on reel number two (the middle reel), we count five cherries; on reel number three, we find there are again only two cherries. The *award glass* on the machine shows that one cherry on the payline of the left reel in combination with any symbol other than another cherry on the middle and right reels will pay two coins.

So let's figure out how often, theoretically speaking, we can expect to win on this particular pay combination. There are 2 chances in 22 that a cherry will appear on reel number one, right? On reel number two, we can have any symbol except a cherry. We already know there are 22 symbols on reel number two but 5 of them are cherries, so we subtract 5 from 22. Thus we find we have 17 chances in 22 that a symbol other than a cherry will appear on the second reel. Doing the same thing for reel number three, which has 2 cherries on it, we find we have 20 chances in 22 of a symbol other than a cherry appearing on the payline. Now we can compute our chances like this:

$$2 \times 17 \times 20 = 680$$

Because there are a total of 10,648 different possible outcomes in the cycle, as we've already seen (22 × 22 × 22 = 10,648), we can therefore say that one cherry by itself on the first reel should show up 680 times in the cycle.

Next, let's see how often we can expect 3 cherries to line up on our hypothetical machine over an indefinite period of play. Again, there are 2 chances in 22 that a cherry will appear on the payline on reels one and three, and on the middle reel there are 5 chances in 22 that a cherry will show up. This time we will compute the chances by determining how many times a cherry *will* rather than will not show up on reels two and three. Thus, we must state our chances like this:

$$2 \times 5 \times 2 = 20$$

In other words, the theoretical odds are that in 10,648 plays of the machine, 3 cherries will line up 20 times.

Let's do this just once more. This time we will see how often we should expect to line up three plums. Counting the plums on each reel, we find that reel number one has

5, reel number two has only 1, and reel number three has 10 plums. Our chances are:

$$5 \times 1 \times 10 = 50$$

Three plums should hit 50 times in a cycle of 10,648 plays.

Now you know how the theoretical odds for any given pay combination can be computed. In order to get a complete picture of the slot machine selected for this discussion, we would first need to add up the number of like symbols on each reel, as we have started to do already. This is what our sample machine would look like:

Symbols	Reels		
	#1	#2	#3
Cherries	2	5	2
Oranges	2	3	7
Plums	5	1	10
Bells	10	2	1
Bars	2	10	1
7s	1	1	1

Next, it would be necessary to compute the expected number of hits per cycle for each *pay combination*, just as we started to do above. Here is how that would look:

Pay Combination	Chances Per Reel	Hits
Cherry/Any/Any	2 × 17 × 20 =	680
Any/Any/Cherry	20 × 17 × 2 =	680
Cherry/Cherry/Any	2 × 5 × 20 =	200
Any/Cherry/Cherry	20 × 5 × 2 =	200

Pay Combination	Chances Per Reel	Hits
Cherry/Any/Cherry	2 × 17 × 2 =	68
Cherry/Cherry/Cherry	2 × 5 × 2 =	20
Bar/Orange/Orange	2 × 3 × 7 =	42
Orange/Orange/Bar	2 × 3 × 1 =	6
Orange/Orange/Orange	3 × 2 × 7 =	42
Bar/Plum/Plum	2 × 1 × 10 =	20
Plum/Plum/Bar	5 × 1 × 1 =	5
Plum/Plum/Plum	5 × 1 × 10 =	50
Bar/Bell/Bell	2 × 2 × 1 =	4
Bell/Bell/Bar	10 × 2 × 1 =	20
Bell/Bell/Bell	10 × 2 × 1 =	20
Bar/Bar/Bar	2 × 10 × 1 =	20
7/7/7	1 × 1 × 1 =	1

Now that we know how many times each pay combination could theoretically be expected to hit in the 10,648 cycle, we can compute what is called a *hit frequency*, which refers to how often, on the average, this machine will pay out.

Hit frequency is stated as a percentage and can be determined by adding together the number of expected hits for each pay combination, and then finding the ratio of the sum of the total expected hits to the cycle.

For instance, the total number of expected hits for the pay combinations listed above is 2,078. What percent is 2,078 of 10,648? The answer is 20.7. We can therefore say that our machine will pay out approximately once in every five plays, or 20 percent of the time.

The only other thing we need to know is how much money this machine is going to pay us and how much it is going to keep, or *hold*. In order to figure this, it is first necessary to look at the award glass to see what our machine pays for each separate pay combination. Then the individual pays are multiplied by the expected number of hits so that a total of coins paid out per cycle can be determined. Here is what we would find:

Pay Combination	No. of Coins Awarded	Expected Hits	Total Coins Paid Out
Cherry/Any/Any	2	680	1,360
Any/Any/Cherry	2	680	1,360
Cherry/Cherry/Any	5	200	1,000
Any/Cherry/Cherry	5	200	1,000
Cherry/Any/Cherry	5	68	340
Cherry/Cherry/Cherry	20	20	400
Bar/Orange/Orange	10	42	420
Orange/Orange/Bar	10	6	60
Orange/Orange/Orange	20	42	840
Bar/Plum/Plum	14	20	280
Plum/Plum/Bar	14	5	70
Plum/Plum/Plum	20	50	1,000
Bar/Bell/Bell	18	4	72
Bell/Bell/Bar	18	20	360
Bell/Bell/Bell	20	20	400
Bar/Bar/Bar	50	20	1,000
7/7/7	100	1	100

Adding the coins paid out for each pay combination, we get a grand total of 10,062. This happens to be 94.5 percent of the 10,648 coins required to play a complete cycle (playing one coin at a time). Thus, a casino could truthfully advertise that this machine has an average payback of 94.5 percent.

Does that mean you are going to get back at least 95 percent of all the coins you play into this machine? Not exactly! It would be necessary either to hit the three 7s and every possible pay combination precisely as many times in one cycle as the theoretical odds predict or to play this machine for several days non-stop in order to come close to receiving a 95 percent average payback.

What the payout percentage tells us is how much the machine keeps for the casino. If the machine pays out 94.5 percent, it must then hold 5.5 percent. In other words, over an indefinite period of time the casino would profit by 5-1/2 cents on every dollar played into our machine. Most slot machines will have a hold of between 5 percent and 15 percent.

The thing to remember is that people do not play a slot machine because they want to prove the theoretical odds to themselves. People play slots because they want to beat those odds; they want to win more money than they spend. That's what it's all about. It's what you could win—not lose—that counts.

There is no quick way of telling how many stops a machine has simply by looking at it. If you ask the casino employees, they most likely will tell you they don't know. That's because they are telling the truth, and you shouldn't feel it's some big secret to keep you from finding a good machine. Also, it is my guess that a keyperson or mechanic would be most reluctant to open a machine and count the reel strip symbols for you; that would look suspicious to other customers—and to casino management as well.

Just take your chances. But for the record, a 25-stop machine has a cycle of 15,625 symbol combinations. That's almost half again as many as a 22-stop machine. Hit frequencies could remain about the same, however, for similar machines even though the number of reel stops differs. It's when reel stops get up to the 40s, 50s, and 60s, or into the hundreds (as they do on many of the videos) that the odds on hitting the jackpot can become astronomical. Then, again, the size of the jackpot often is also astronomical, such as is the case on many of the link progressives.

In addition to the number of stops, the number of reels also affects the odds. Our sample machine in this chapter had three reels, but it is not uncommon to see four-, five- or even six-reel slot machines. Although a majority of slots still have only three reels, consider for a moment what adding a fourth reel does to the machine's cycle. A 22-stop, three-reel machine has, as you know, a 10,648 cycle (22 × 22 × 22 = 10,648). Add the fourth reel, and the number of different possible symbol combinations jumps to 234,256 (22 × 22 × 22 × 22 = 234,256). A fifth reel on this same machine would have a cycle of over 5,000,000!

What this may mean is that if you are playing a five-reel progressive slot, your odds of hitting the big jackpot could be less than 1 in 5,000,000. But don't dispair, the odds can be even worse, especially on some machines offering jackpots that approach or surpass $1,000,000 for a three-coin wager. You should only choose to play these machines in hopes of being lucky, or just being in the right place at the right time. Naturally, the likelihood of hitting a jackpot is much better on a machine on which the most you can win is only 30+ times the amount of the wager instead of 300,000 times.

As you can see, there's more to the operation of a slot machine than just "around and around she goes . . .," and yet there is a lot of truth also in that little jingle.

Now that you are acquainted with how slots pay off,

it would next be appropriate to talk about the various machines you will find available for you to play—which are the "good" ones, how many coins you should play, what you should look for, things like that.

CHAPTER 4

The Basics About Playing Today's Slots

Because of an explosion in the popularity of slot machines and the fantastic advances in electronic technology in recent years, many new slot games have appeared in today's casinos. It is no longer a matter of walking up to a slot machine, inserting a coin, and pulling the handle. For one thing, many new games do not have handles; some of the new slots require that you indicate how you want to play by depressing buttons before the outcome of the game can be determined.

Even if you take time to read the instructions on the machine glass, the really important information about playing one machine instead of another will not be obvious. That's why an understanding of the basic types of machines available for you and some of the important particulars of each type are absolutely necessary if you do not wish to just throw your money away. Trust me, there is no more important information in this book than you will find right here.

MECHANICAL OR ELECTRO-MECHANICAL SLOT MACHINES

Still the most familiar and common machine found in the casino is the conventional *mechanical* or more advanced *electro-mechanical* slot machine. This is the kind of slot we all know about, right? Wrong! Most players recognize this type of slot machine because it looks like a slot machine should; it has reels that spin around when the handle is pulled. Where the reels stop determines if you win or not—simple.

Well, as you will soon see, casinos make millions and millions because people assume they understand how a familiar-looking slot machine works. Years ago, capitalizing on the appeal of these machines, slot machine designers began making it possible to win and lose on more than one payline each time the handle is pulled. This means more than one coin can, or in some cases *must*, be played at a time if you are to get paid, even though you have lined up a winning combination of symbols on one of the paylines.

Single-Coin Slot Machines

There still are, however, some machines around that only accept one coin per play. They may not be found in the newer, larger casinos, but some of the smaller clubs still have a good selection. These *single-coin slots* are the older-looking machines in mostly nickel, dime, and quarter denominations. They may have skinny little reels that spin and jerk to a stop with a clang. Single-coin nickel denomination machines often pay jackpots of $7.50, with $15.00 maximum.

Some customers feel these are the only true slot machines left in this world and will play only where these machines are still in service. Playing the single-coin machines can provide hours of fun; and while it is unlikely you will make a killing, you can often enjoy losing slowly.

Multiple-Coin Slot Machines

Multiple-coin slot machines accept or require more than one coin per play and exist in a variety of configurations. Multiple-coin machines that the industry calls *multipliers* normally have a single payline across the reel glass; in other words, winning combinations have to line up on the center line. But, depending on the machine, you can play from one to six or more coins at a time. Most multiplier slot machines today, however, accept either three or five coins maximum per play. The idea is that each additional coin inserted increases proportionately the amount you can win on a payable combination of symbols.

Where does the multiplier idea fit in, you ask? Good question! Often, but not always, a bonus amount is paid if you win on the highest jackpot symbols (usually 7s)—provided that the maximum number coins the machine will accept were inserted.

Let's take a closer look at this. If you are playing a three-reel, three-coin quarter multiplier (casinos call this type of machine a "25¢, 3-coin multi") and you line up three bars, here's what you might win. With only one quarter played, the machine would pay 50 quarters; with two quarters played, you'd win 100 quarters; and with three coins played, you'd get paid 150 quarters. In other words, each additional coin played proportionately increased by 50 coins what you won, but nothing was actually multiplied.

Now, however, let's say you lined up three 7s and played only one coin. You should have received a 100-coin pay. Had you played two coins, you would have received 200 coins; and for three coins played, you'd have won 600 coins. Note that the three-coin payoff is three times the amount paid for two coins played. If that same jackpot had only increased proportionately (as it did for the bars), you would have received just 300 coins. So you can see that the highest jackpot, for 7s, is multiplied, so to speak, if the maximum coins are played. In effect, you received a 300-coin bonus for playing three quarters instead of only one or two when the 7s lined up.

What does this complicated explanation about multipliers tell you? For one thing, if the machine you select pays a jackpot bonus for playing the maximum coins possible, you will be cheating yourself when you hit the jackpot if you play fewer coins than the maximum. It is important to remember that not all multipliers pay a jackpot bonus, though, so look closely at the award glass on your machine before deciding how many coins you wish to play.

Multipliers that do not pay a jackpot bonus have the advantage that they can be played as single-coin machines (one coin at a time), and you incur no penalty if you hit the jackpot. If your objective is to play as long as possible on as little money as possible, playing one coin a time on a non-bonus jackpot multiplier may be a good idea.

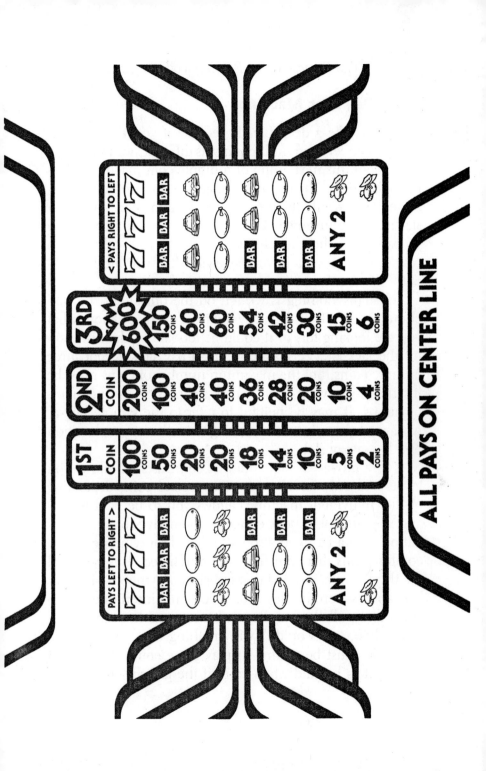

ALL PAYS ON CENTER LINE

Buy-a-Pay Slot Machines

Now take a deep breath because if you thought that trying to understand multipliers was difficult, wait until you hear about this next group of multiple coin machines. It is my opinion that the *buy-a-pay* machine confuses more customers and results in more dissatisfaction than any other slot machine invented. Of course, if I owned a casino I'd probably love these machines because, as you will see, it is easy to not win on a buy-a-pay even when you hit the jackpot.

Usually nothing is written on the outside of the machine to identify it as a buy-a-pay. You must know what you are looking for, or it could be too late by the time you hit the jackpot. Very simply, buy-a-pay slots accept three or more coins, but the maximum number of coins must be inserted if you want to win on all the possible symbol combinations. It may be helpful to refer to the sample buy-a-pay award glass illustration during the following explanation of a buy-a-pay slot.

In a buy-a-pay slot, the first coin inserted allows you to be paid only for cherries. The second coin, depending on the individual machine, allows you to be paid for oranges, plums, and bells either by themselves or in combination with a bar; you also will be paid for winning cherry combinations that your first coin purchased. It is not until the third coin is inserted that the jackpot symbols—bars, or bars and 7s—are in play. So, if you only insert one or two coins and pull the handle, and three bars line up on the center line, you wouldn't win anything.

You must be willing to play three coins at a time if you want to be paid when you hit the jackpot on a buy-a-

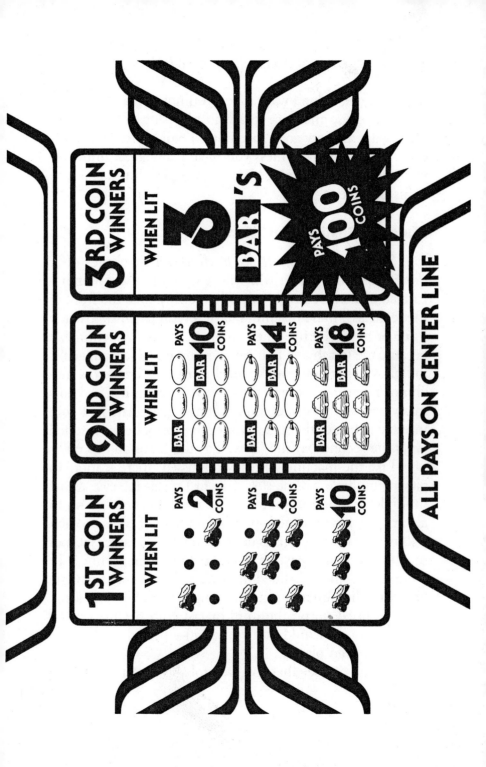

pay machine. I don't want to tell you not to play these machines because many people who play slots regularly feel buy-a-pays are very good machines. I will advise you, however, to be careful. Unless you have really great hunches, you would be well advised to always play the maximum coins possible.

Multiple Payline Slot Machines

Simply stated, *multiple payline* slot machines offer more than one way to win with each pull of the handle. Instead of a single or center payline only across the front of the reel glass, these machines have several paylines, usually three or five. The five-line machines are easily identifiable because the fourth and fifth paylines run on a diagonal across the glass. This slot is nicknamed a *five-line criss-cross* machine. You can choose by the number of coins inserted how many paylines you want to play at one time. The first coin inserted activates the first payline, the second coin inserted plays the second payline (as well as the first), and so on.

Like the machines already discussed, there is more to playing multiple-payline slots than first meets the eye. Many multiple-payline machines are set up to encourage you to always play the maximum possible number of coins on each pull of the handle. This is done by offering a larger jackpot on the last coin's payline than on the other paylines. In other words, three 7s lined up on the second coin's payline of a three-line quarter machine might pay $50. The same three 7s lined up on the third or last coin payline on the same machine would pay you $250—provided all three coins had been played.

So you can see that you are probably better off playing

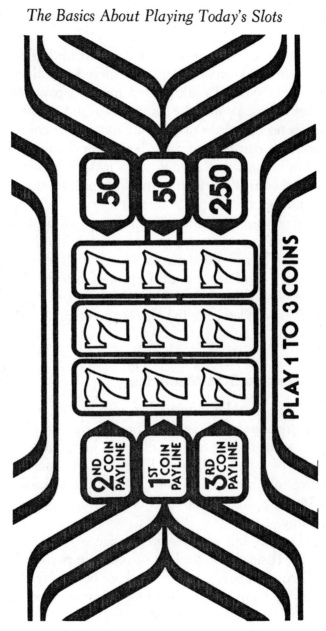

the maximum coins possible when your multiple-line machine offers a jackpot bonus. But there is, as always, a big "however": Not all multiple payline slots pay a bonus for the last payline jackpot. Be sure to check this out first because there is no benefit to playing the maximum coins possible unless you can receive a big bonus for doing so. As with the muiltipliers that do not pay a jackpot bonus, you can play one coin at a time in a multiple payline machine that does not offer a jackpot bonus, conserve your money, and still be at your machine when the cocktail waitress makes her next trip by to serve complimentary drinks (provided you are in a casino that serves free cocktails to slot players). This way, you have the satisfaction of knowing that if you are not winning, at least you can drink for free! Well, almost free, that is. (Please see the chapter on etiquette and tipping in casinos.)

Progressive Slot Machines

The entire slot industry has been revolutionized by the acceptance and popularity of progressive slot play. When you read in the newspaper of some lucky soul winning a jackpot of a half-million dollars or more, there is a good chance (like almost 100 percent) that the jackpot occurred on a progressive slot carousel or individual progressive slot machine.

Terrific, but what's a progressive, you ask? *Progressive* slots are basically multipliers or multiple-payline machines (as discussed above), but the jackpot bonus for playing the maximum coins possible in a progressive increases each time the machines are played until the jackpot is hit. In other words, a small percentage of every coin inserted into a progressive slot will be added to the jackpot award, and a sign on and/or above the machine will continually be updated so you can always see what you can win. When the jackpot is hit, a minimum new jackpot is established and the progressive process starts all over.

Although progressives may be installed on various types of slot games, our discussion at this point will be limited only to those progressives that apply to reel-type slot machines.

Progressive slots are set up in two ways. The older and more common progressive slot is an individual freestanding machine. It can be found either by itself among the non-progressive slots or on a stand with other progressive slots, although the machines are not connected to each other in any way.

The more recent setup, made possible by computer technology, is called the *link progressive*. Here, individual machines are hooked together to one central jackpot that increases when any of the individual machines are played. The last coin or last-line jackpot hit on any one of the hooked-together individual machines wins the progressive award provided the maximum coins possible were played. It's when six or ten or twenty or more individual machines are linked to each other and are in constant play that the progressive jackpot award rather quickly reaches a sky-high figure. People who never before played slots because the action wasn't big enough have in recent years moved away from the table games and are now pulling handles. Link progressive slots are very big business.

There is much good to be said for the freestanding individual progressive slots, too. Most of them offer two instead of just one progressive jackpot. That is, two separate jackpots progress alternately as the machine is played, and the player stands a chance to win either one of them. The thing to look for is the machine with the largest jackpots for its particular coin denomination and the number of coins needed per play to win. Of course, the number of reels on the machines you are comparing must be the same. Also, be sure the progressive jackpot is larger than the highest regular jackpot of any non-progressive machine of the same denomination and that it requires the same number of coins to be played.

Personally, I believe that any three-line, three-reel freestanding progressive with a jackpot of two or three times more than a corresponding non-progressive slot would be a super-good machine to play. This would provide an opportunity to win a substantial sum of money and an even bigger thrill should you get lucky and hit the jackpot. Unless you are having serious bad luck, you will probably receive numerous small pays which, if you recycle that money back into the machine, will allow you to stay at this machine quite a while. The longer you can stay on the machine the better your chances of hitting the jackpot, which will have been growing larger all the time you've been playing.

But let's say you want to play "big time." You would rather win a couple hundred thousand dollars or more, or nothing at all. You, my friend, are ready for one of the many dollar (or frequently quarter) giant link progressive carousels just waiting for brave souls like yourself. You will be playing the toughest odds to be found anywhere—and if your luck isn't good, you will spend money like it is going out of style. Nevertheless, more often than not, I've seen players walk up to one of these giant progressives with $20 or $30 in their hands and walk away with a quarter of a million or better.

In fact, that exactly sums up my feelings on how to play these super-jackpot progressives. Start out with a specific, comfortable sum of funds and say to yourself, "I'll play on this until it runs out. If I win, great. If I lose, well, I took a chance and I'll try again another time."

If you do win, you'd better be ready for the consequences. Depending on the amount you've won, you will be interviewed, photographed, and interviewed again and photographed again. You'll be visited by casino executives, gaming agents, and the general public who will want to touch you in hopes that your good luck will rub off. After all of this, the machine you were playing will be inspected with a fine-tooth comb to assure the casino executives and gaming regulators that you were an honest winner. All in all, winning a super jackpot can be a real ordeal. Granted, it would be a profitable ordeal; but you should, nevertheless, be prepared. Some people handle all this quite well—they just ask the casino to keep pouring the champagne while they sit at their ringing machine, and soon all the commotion becomes no problem whatsoever!

There are a couple more things to know about when you hit a "big one." On some progressive carousels, a choice of bonus prizes is offered in addition to the cash jackpot. You may get to choose, for instance, a trip around the world, your own personal airplane, a new motorhome, or other luxury vehicle. In most cases, you must make your choice immediately as it is figured into the value of your jackpot for tax purposes.

At the present time, most super-large jackpots are paid in one lump sum by check, or by a combination of cash and check. Future giant jackpots may be paid in installments so as to discourage slot cheats and provide the winner a better opportunity to financially plan his or her future.

Above all else, if you do have the good fortune to win a bundle, please be polite and cooperative. Remember, this is supposed to be the thrill of a lifetime. Don't make it a nightmare. Also, you will be surprised how much more friendly and helpful the casino personnel can become if you show some class.

Jackpot-Only or All-Jackpot Slot Machines

Slot machines that pay only jackpots are actually just multipliers or multiple-line machines that omit the smaller pays in favor of less frequent but larger payouts. For example, one quarter, five-coin multiplier, jackpot-only machine has only three pay combinations. With one coin played, you can only win $5, $25, or $50; with five coins played, you could receive $25, $125, or a last-coin bonus jackpot of $500. In other words, any payout of 18 coins or less that you would expect to receive somewhat often on regular machines is eliminated on the all-jackpot machines. These small pays are omitted by simply removing all the pay combinations except jackpot symbols from the reels of the machine. You can instantly recognize a jackpot-only machine the minute you walk up to it by the fact that there are a lot of blank spots on the reels where a regular machine would have cherries, oranges, dollar signs, or some other symbol.

Is there any advantage to playing a jackpot-only slot instead of a regular machine? No. It's just a matter of personal choice. The regular machine will put fewer coins in the tray more often; the jackpot-only machine will put more coins in the tray less often, that's all. For what it's worth, I think it's more fun to get a few coins paid out frequently than a bunch only once in a while. All things being equal (such as same hold, same number of reel stops, etc.), both the regular machines and the jackpot-only machines will pay out about the same over an extended period of time.

The "Berthas"

This final category of conventional slot machines is almost not worth mentioning, but in the cause of thoroughness I'll slip it in here. *Berthas*, as in "Big Bertha," are giant, oversized machines sprinkled here and there around the casino. They are not very popular now, but they can still be found in pretty good number. Some are multipliers; some are multiple-line; some are progressives. All are fun to drop a few coins into, but basically they are "turkeys." If I were you, I wouldn't play them very long. You can usually do better elsewhere.

VIDEO SLOT MACHINES

Video slot machines are tomorrow's slot machines today. Videos, they say, are the wave of the future. They're probably right. It's been said that the whole generation of youth is being primed for video gaming through the popularity of video arcades and home video game equipment. Whereas slot machines today are strictly a game of chance (of course, your chances are better if you know what you are doing—thus, this book), future slot games could very well include elements of skill as well as chance. By skill we mean something other than simply making intelligent choices based upon knowledge of how a game is played.

Video draw poker machines are a good example. Your

knowledge of the game may help you to win, but possessing great physical dexterity or eye-hand coordination or something of that sort does not improve your chances. The debate about allowing skill to become a factor in automated wagering has already heated up and will no doubt become hotter in the future.

But, back to present-day video games themselves. In addition to the video poker machines there are also video 21 (blackjack) machines, video keno, video versions of regular reel-type slot machines, and a whole host of other video specialty machines.

In general, it is possible to talk about most all video slots at one time. Except for certain specific features on some of the machines or the add-on technology of other special games, videos of all kinds are more similar than they are different. To start with, video slot machines have far fewer moving parts than do mechanical or electro-mechanical slots. Videos employ 100 percent computer-age technology: microprocessors, chips, memories—all those good things we hear about all the time and don't understand.

Of course, on all video slots you are really watching a TV screen that shows you a picture of reels spinning around or playing cards being dealt to you or some such thing. Most of the newer videos also play little songs or make funny noises when you insert your coins or receive a pay from the machine. Some of these games actually talk to you; and most of them give you written instructions, information, or encouragement.

It is not uncommon for some videos to play themselves when no one else is playing them; this is called a *self-shill* feature. Besides attracting attention, the self-shill feature permits customers to see how the game is played before sitting down to spend their own money. Sitting down, incidentally, is another common characteristic of the video slot era. Manufacturers of videos often sell not only the machine itself but the stand on which it is installed; and attached to the stand is a comfortable swivel chair.

What are videos like to play? Does all that computer stuff take the fun out of it? Are videos "smart" machines on which no one can possibly hope to win? The answer is: Videos can be lots of fun to play, and you can be as lucky playing a video slot as you could be playing anything else.

But, it's up to you. If you are a traditionalist and like only what you are used to, you may not care too much for these new games. On the other hand, if you thought playing slots was always boring, video poker or video horse race or whatever may be a real turn-on. It is true that videos are "smart" machines, but that does not mean there's a little brain inside them that says, "OK, I've taken in this amount of money; now I can afford to give a little of it back."

Like all legal slot machines, the videos also operate on random selection. What occurs is strictly chance, and no single future outcome of a game can be determined by what has previously occurred. That means if you hit a jackpot this time, your chances of hitting it again are just as good as ever, theoretically speaking. (For a better understanding of this, please refer back to Chapter 3, "How Slots Pay Off.")

There *are* some differences between the conventional reel-type slots and their video reel-type counterparts. The video version will usually have more pay symbol combinations, for one thing. That means you can be paid for lining up symbols that on a regular non-video slot would pay nothing. This is possible due to the greater number of stops programmed into most of these video machines.

Another difference between videos and regular reel-type slots is that the video tends to more consistently maintain its hold. To say it another way, the conventional machine is more likely to be a temporary loser for the casino. This is probably the reason that serious slot gamblers tend to prefer the conventional mechanical/electro-mechanicals to the videos.

Video Poker Machines

No other single category of slots is more popular at the present time than the *video poker machines*. Some people are literally hooked on them. It isn't unusual to see customers stand in line to play these machines. There are both the standard and progressive applications of the video poker game, and one is just as popular as the other.

As with most slots, nickels, quarters, and dollars are the most popular denominations for the poker machines. I don't know what it is about this game, but you better look out, because these machines can mesmerize you. It's quite relaxing to focus your attention on the blue screen in front of you as you draw and discard hand upon colorful hand, game after game.

On the same amount of money, you could probably play a poker machine longer than any reel-type machine. Said another way, it probably takes longer to lose playing video poker. But unless you hit a royal flush or at least a few four-of-a-kinds or better in the course of the time you are playing, don't expect to get rich playing video poker. Yes, you can make money at it, but it's mostly the enjoyment of playing as well as picking up a few bucks that makes it such a popular game.

Video Blackjack (21)

There are a couple of important differences you should know about between the video version of blackjack and a real, live game. A *blackjack machine* (blackjack and 21 are the same game) uses only one 52-card deck, but the deck is shuffled electronically before each and every hand played. Card counting is, therefore, impossible. Another difference is that on some but not all blackjack machines the player loses on pushes (ties); the newer machines, however, will return your money on a push, as is done in most table games of blackjack.

These machines are fun to play for a while but definitely lack the hypnotizing effect of the poker machines. Give them a try, and you can decide for yourself.

Keno Machines

Keno machines can be surprisingly entertaining. They are not going to mesmerize you like the pokers; but they keep your visit to the slot department from becoming dull— they offer a little variety. One major difference from live keno is that machine keno takes a lot less money to play. But guess what? You can easily play machine keno ten or twenty times faster than real keno—so which game will likely end up being the more costly in the long run? You can answer that one.

The other side of the coin is that if live keno was too slow to keep you interested, video keno could be the answer. Finally, you can only play straight keno on a machine; there is no provision for a "way ticket."

The "Revolutionary" Videos

The "revolutionary" videos have been made possible only by the technology of the electronic revolution and the computer age. One of the more common new video games at the present time is *horse racing*. It works something like this. Actual races from a track are photographed or recorded on a video laser disk. The disk, which can store many separate races, is then installed in the horse race machine.

When you insert your coins, the machine will randomly select a race and provide you with a video read-out of the horses and their odds. You then bet on one or more horses to win, push the start button, and the race is played for you on a TV monitor built into the machine. You get paid according to what the odds were if your horse wins. No show or place bets are possible on the machines I've seen.

A variety of other unique video games are being tried these days, but there is no telling what tomorrow will bring. Because of such developments, automated gambling within the casino may never be the same. No doubt there's an exciting future in video gaming. Maybe someday people will say they can remember when casinos used to have slot machines with funny reels that spun around with little pictures of fruit on them. When three pieces of the same kind of fruit lined up in the window of the machine, you would win. Imagine that!

NOVELTY GAMING DEVICES

These new machines, *novelty gaming devices*, are neither videos nor reel-type slot machines. Several varieties of one of these games, the *pusher-paddle machine*, are on the market and have been well received by the public. Part of the appeal may be that the internal workings of this particular game are entirely open to view through a large glass cover on the machine. You can watch what becomes of your coins as you play them.

It works like this: When you insert a coin, it is mechanically tossed up into the interior of the machine. Each coin has a chance to do several things that can result in your receiving a pay. First, it could fall into one of the several little baskets or openings on the back of the machine's interior. Each of these baskets or openings is worth a specific sum of money, perhaps $5 or $10, which the machine would then pay to you.

Second, if your coin misses an opening or basket, it then can land on one of several little shelves along with a lot of other coins that have previously landed there. On each shelf are a series of pusher paddles that act like a snow-plow. If your coin lands on the shelf just right, the plow pushes it into the other coins, some of which then spill over the edge of the shelf and eventually end up in the payout tray of your machine. If all goes well, your one coin could cause five or six or more other coins to fall off the little shelf, and thus you would become a winner. You will not be able to retire on what you win from one of these machines, I guarantee you. Play them for a little diversion.

KNOW WHAT YOU ARE DOING

Now you can understand why, as we said at the beginning of this chapter, it's no longer only a matter of walking up to a slot machine, inserting a coin, and pulling the handle. You have to know what you are doing if you reasonably expect to have fun and want to improve your chances of winning something.

You should now be able to find a slot game to match your playing objective. If you want to become instantly rich, pick one of the giant jackpot link progressives. If you only want to win enough to pay for your vacation or get the kitchen remodeled, look for an individual freestanding progressive machine with the right-size jackpot. (Be sure to use the selection criteria as indicated in this chapter.)

If you want to relax and get away from it all, play one of the video poker games. If you want to watch people or listen to the live casino entertainment, pick a nickel or dime machine near an aisle or next to the show lounge. And so on.

Do remember several things. Look at the machine carefully before playing it. Read every word on the machine—take nothing for granted. If there is something you don't understand, ask the slot attendant.

One thing to look for is whether or not your machine has a *credit feature*. If it does, you may not immediately be paid in coins when you win something. Instead, what you've won will first be credited on the machine. Then you have the option of pressing a *collect button* to receive payments for the credits, or you can use the winning credits to further play the machine without inserting more coins. A numerical display or meter on the machine will indicate the amount the machine owes you. These credit machines confuse a lot of people, and quite a few slot players walk away from the machines that owe them money. The credit feature is not a new idea, but it is becoming increasingly prevalent. Always be sure to check for this feature before playing any machine.

Also, be sure to notice little signs that read, "It Is the Player's Responsibility to be Certain All Coins Inserted Have Registered in the Machine Before the Handle is Pulled." This is important. Even if you do insert the maximum coins that the machine will take, if each coin has not registered properly as indicated by a corresponding light on the front of the machine, you may not be paid for what you may have won.

You also may notice a sign in fine print that reads, "Malfunction Voids All Plays." If you have any suspicion that your machine may not be working properly, report it. You are only hurting your own chances of winning if you do not report a malfunction.

Be sure you know what a jackpot looks like, so you don't play one off accidentally and then not get paid. You would be surprised how many people hit jackpots and do not know what they won until someone tells them. Because the jackpot bell frequently will fail to ring (if your machine has a bell!), it is extra important to pay attention.

Also, be sure you know which symbols represent the highest possible jackpot on your machine and if the machine itself pays that jackpot or if a slot attendant has to pay it. Very often, when jackpots are only partially paid by the machine, the unwary slot player will scoop up the coins from the tray and walk away, never to receive the remaining (and much larger) winnings that would have been paid by an attendant. On the largest jackpots, especially the progressives, the slot machine will usually pay nothing, and the player must wait for the jackpot to be hand-paid.

Once you do hit a jackpot that is partially or totally paid by an attendant, do not leave your machine for even one second. Do not insert any more coins or even touch the handle. Do not allow anyone else to touch your machine. Until all your jackpot money is in your hand, do not take your eyes off your machine. At the appropriate time, a slot employee will ask you to play off your jackpot (that is, insert another coin and pull the handle) in order that the payment transaction can be completed. Only after you have done this can you relax.

And, finally, why not quit while you are ahead, or at least put some of your winnings aside. After a good win, celebrate and enjoy the feeling of being lucky. Some people, once they've won something, become greedy and end up stuffing everything back into the machine. Quit a winner, even if for only an hour or two. If, after taking a break and congratulating yourself on your good fortune, you decide to try your luck again, more power to you!

CHAPTER 5

Watch Out for the IRS

Here comes the Internal Revenue Service. Is this another myth? When someone wins a big jackpot, does the tax man get you? It's not a myth, it's a reality! Maybe the tax man (IRS employee) does not appear in person at the side of your slot machine, but the casino is required to do the IRS's work for them. This means that the casino must help the IRS make sure that slot winners report their winnings above a certain level and subsequently pay taxes on those winnings.

The casino accomplishes its task by completing and filing with the Internal Revenue Service a form called a "W-2G." One such form is submitted to the IRS on every slot winner of a jackpot of $1,200 and over. The W-2G form is somewhat similar to an ordinary W-2 form, which most of us receive from our employers; it shows how much we've earned over a given period of time.

For the most part, slot winnings, as far as reportable income is concerned, are just like income received from your job. As far as the IRS is concerned, what you normally

59

earn in a year will be increased by the amount of your slot winnings.

Next question. Are taxes taken out before the jackpot is paid off, or does the winner get paid the full amount of the jackpot? If the winner is a permanent United States resident, with the proper identification, no tax is deducted from the winnings at the time the jackpot is paid. But if the winner is a foreign resident (lives outside the United States), tax is withheld in an amount determined according to country of residence. Except for Canadians, most foreign-resident winners would be subject to a withholding of 30 percent from the jackpot proceeds. Canadians incur a withholding of 15 percent on any jackpot of $1,200 or more.

Is it necessary to give the casino your Social Security number and be able to provide appropriate ID? Yes! If you win a taxable jackpot, you will be required to supply a couple of forms of identification. The usual kinds of ID such as a driver's license and credit card will do fine. Of course, you must have a Social Security number as well. Unfortunately, many people do not really expect to win anything very big when visiting a casino and thus leave their identification in the hotel room—or worse, at home. If you do that, you could receive a receipt for your newly acquired wealth instead of the real thing—check or cash—and have to come back later with appropriate ID to get paid.

Slot players often ask, "Since the law requires that my slot winnings be reported as part of my gross income, can I deduct what I have lost?" The official answer is yes, you can. That is, if you itemize deductions on your federal income tax return, you are entitled to deduct losses to the extent of the amount you report having won. However, these losses must be claimed as a miscellaneous deduction and not simply subtracted from your winnings. Furthermore, should your losses exceed what you've won during a taxable year, there is no provision for carrying the excess over to subsequent years.

Of course, it is necessary to be able to substantiate the losses you claim. This may be the most difficult part of the job. All slot winners claiming a deduction must show satisfactory evidence of their losses. How can you do that playing a slot machine? After all, after each pull of the handle the machine doesn't issue you a receipt that says, "Sorry, you lost. Save this slip for tax purposes."

If you keep a *diary* of all gaming transactions and can provide corroborating documentation, the IRS will usually accept the diary as evidence of any losses. One possible format of a slot player's diary is shown here, but the diary can take any form. (Additional pages of this sample diary are provided in the Appendix.) It should include all the obvious information, such as where you were playing, the date and time, the floor number or location of the slot machine you played, and, of course, whether you won or lost at the end of the time you were playing. You should also list people with you, other witnesses, names of cashiers or changepersons who waited on you, and anything else you can think of that might substantiate your entries. Taking time to add all the miscellaneous comments is most important.

In addition, the IRS will want to see all records, charge slips, cashed checks, and personal documentation that will support such a claim. Supporting documentation may include hotel or motel bills, losing keno tickets establishing that you were actually in the casino on the date you claim you incurred losses on slots, casino credit slips, airline tickets or gasoline receipts, etc.

SLOT PLAYER'S WIN-AND-LOSS DIARY

Date	Casino Name and Location	Machine Number	Hours Played	Coin Bought	Coin Returned	Won or <Lost>	Additional Information: Witnesses, employee names and positions, other miscellaneous details.

Also, some casinos will have their employees fill out a *gaming loss statement* for you. This form, which states that you lost a specific sum of money, can be used as supporting evidence for your deduction. Many casinos, however, do not have the ability to substantiate a slot player's losses and may not be willing to issue a loss statement. Ask ahead of time if someone is available to confirm any losses that you might incur and if a loss statement would be available to document such losses.

Finally, if you're serious about hitting it big, it may be a good idea to give some thought ahead of time to what you plan to do with the money. You may not be so lucky as to win your big jackpot in January or February and have all year long to decide which are your best investments so far as tax purposes are concerned. After all, with $500,000 or $1,000,000 hanging out of your hip pocket, you got responsibilities! Good luck. I wish I had your problems.

CHAPTER 6

You and the Law

Is a discussion about you and the law regarding slot play really necessary? Perhaps not, but in the interest of providing the most thorough treatment of the subject, a look at how some people inadvertently (or otherwise) get into trouble playing slots is included here.

Before detailing some actual "no-no's," let's talk first about a couple of general attitudes that people sometimes express about casinos and the activity of gambling therein. There are those who feel the casino is a place where the odds are stacked against them in a sort of dishonest way. The important element here is the mistaken idea that it is dishonesty instead of economic reality that results in a *profit margin* for the casinos in the games they offer. This profit margin (the odds favoring the casino) is as little as 1/2 or 1 percent on even-money bets at some table games, and, overall, is lower than many people think.

From our previous discussion about how slot machines pay off, you have seen that the profit casinos make on these games is between 5 and 15 percent. This is certainly not a ripoff, for the profit margins of most businesses today are almost always greater than 15 percent. Yet, a certain number of people will walk through the doors of casinos every day thinking that the place is going to try to cheat them and so they must be on their guard.

And a minority of these people will take this thinking even one step further. Not only do they think the casino is out to cheat them, they feel they have a right or obligation to themselves to try to cheat the casino first. They may cheat only in a small way, like telling a casino employee their slot machine didn't pay them all the money it should have after stuffing a handful of coins into their pocket. No big deal, right? Well, it's "no big deals" like that and a few others I will mention that can result in a loused-up visit or vacation.

First, just in case you have any doubt in your mind about the honesty of the casinos or their employees, I want to state for the record that no other business I know of spends more money or time policing itself than does the gaming industry. This means that there is no conspiracy to keep you from winning when a slot mechanic services your machine if you have a problem. If a floor supervisor tells you that you did not win when you think you should have, that supervisor is not trying to save the casino money. He or she is telling you the truth and would much perfer to see you win and have a good time.

Employees in casinos do not take some kind of loyalty oath that says they will always work to favor the house at the expense of the customer. That would be foolish and poor business, for one thing. Secondly, where are employees to be found these days who would feel that kind of loyalty to their employers anyway?

Slot Machine Cheating

Some of the ways slot players can get themselves into trouble may originally be unintentional. The most common violation of laws regarding slot play has already been mentioned—it is informally called *claiming* and can occur in a variety of situations in which the players falsely claim that the slot machine has malfunctioned. The most obvious ploy is stating that they have more money coming because the machine didn't pay them at all or that it only paid part of what they should have won. In other words, the customers falsely state that they received a *no pay* or a *short pay*.

Of course it is possible for no pays and short pays to occur on any slot machine. If this should happen to you, just call a casino employee, who will get a mechanic to help you. You don't have to worry about being accused of cheating. For one thing, an inspection of the machine will usually confirm that you are correct about what happened. Secondly, even when the machine offers no evidence of not paying or of short paying, and if it is only a question of a few coins, many casinos will give you the benefit of the doubt. So don't be afraid to speak up if you have this kind of problem; it's when the same customer reports the same problem over and over again that the casino becomes suspicious.

Another kind of claiming has to do with customers who insist that a slot machine they were *not* playing owes them money. It works like this. These dishonest players will find a machine on which someone else previously won, took the money, and walked away without playing off the jackpot. Then, pointing to the winning symbols the previous player had lined up on the payline, these customers will now claim they were playing that machine but "no money came out." Even though the machine will show that the real winner was paid, these players will insist they are the winner and thus have money coming. If you try this approach a few times, don't be surprised if big trouble and unfriendly faces show up.

Next comes the more overt and obvious attempt to play a slot machine for free by inserting foreign coins or slugs, better known as *slugging*. The amateur cheat's most popular practice is using foreign coins of a size similar to US coins. The serious slot cheat will use non-magnetic washers or most commonly will make or acquire lead slugs the size of dollar coins and tokens. The really hard-core "slugger" will counterfeit actual casino dollar tokens, a few of which look almost like the real thing. Any persons observed and caught slugging a slot machine, even if they claim only to be seeing if it would work or just fooling around, stand a very good chance of being arrested. Anyone thinking of giving it a try ought to think again. This is not the way to win at playing slots!

By the way, almost no one tries it these days, but *stringing* a slot machine is not feasible for several reasons. Stringing means taping, tying, gluing, or otherwise affixing a string or fine wire to a coin and then inserting and retracting it from the machine in order to get free plays. Cheating in this fashion has become impractical due to anti-cheat devices in the machines as well as the fact that it's hard to string a machine without being seen. A person would have to be pretty stupid to give this a try.

Finally, there's *silvermining*, which may not be exactly a form of cheating but might qualify as the next thing to it. Silvermining is the activity of looking for stray coins inadvertently left in the tray of slot machines or dropped on the floor by other customers. You're not a silverminer if you just pick up a coin or two you find on the floor or in a slot tray, but it does become a problem if you make it a near full-time occupation. Being a silverminer is definitely not a good idea.

Rules, Regulations, and Laws

Not all laws regarding the play of slot machines deal with just cheating. What happens when a machine malfunctions and the casino informs you that the jackpot you just hit is not valid? What happens if you claim that you played the maximum number of coins but the machine shows otherwise, and you do not get paid for what you won? There are gaming laws as well as casino rules and regulations pertaining to those kinds of matters, and many more such situations. It would be impossible to list all the possible problems that might occur, but in general there are a couple of things to know.

As discussed in Chapter 4, many, if not all, casinos place little signs on each slot machine that caution you to "Be Certain All Coins Are Registered Before Pulling Handle." There are a half-dozen or more variations of that warning, but all mean the same thing: Don't claim after you win something that you played more coins than the machine has recorded. People say all the time, "I played three coins—I can't help it if your stupid machine doesn't work." For the most part, a malfunction will void the play, and the wager (your three coins, for example) will be returned. That's all. The three bars showing on the payline and the hundred dollars it would have paid are not subject to negotiation when the machine does not indicate that you inserted the maximum number of coins. The best advice is if all your coins didn't register on the machine when you inserted them, don't pull the handle—call someone first.

Because slot machines are subject to malfunctions just like any other kind of electrical or mechanical device, both the player and the operator (the casino) have a responsibility in the matter. It is expected that the player will not play a machine that has an obvious malfunction and will report that malfunction to a casino employee. The casino, of course, has an obligation to allow only properly working machines to remain in service and to remove from service or fix any slot machine that is not functioning properly.

You can usually tell very quickly if a slot machine isn't working properly. Some of the more obvious things to look for are reels that do not spin at all, spin poorly, or don't come to a stop correctly. If the machine doesn't pay or it pays too much or too little, there is no doubt a problem. It is always best to call it to an employee's attention. You, the customer, will be thanked and treated with respect, which will make for more enjoyment than would an argument or dispute later on.

It's just like anything else—play by the rules and have a good time. Having fun is what it's supposed to be all about, so make that the number one priority.

CHAPTER 7

Slot Player Rules Of Conduct and Etiquette

Because it isn't every day that a player visits a casino, taking time to learn the rules of proper etiquette isn't the first thing you think about just prior to robbing the piggy bank and heading out the door. Most people probably wouldn't even know that rules of polite conduct for slot players exist unless those rules were brought to their attention.

Everyone knows, of course, that the waiter or waitress at a restaurant expects a tip from the customer at the end of the meal. And it's no surprise that the hotel bellperson who carries luggage to a guest's room also expects a gratuity for his or her service. But slot players often do not know when it is appropriate to acknowledge those casino people who have provided cordial assistance and service. If you are thinking right now that you would just as soon remain in the dark on this subject, read no further. You cannot be considered impolite or unappreciative if you truthfully do not know that certain rules of conduct for slot players even exist.

How Many Machines Can You Play?

Slot player etiquette pertains to more than gratuities, however. For instance, many slot customers do not know what is considered the proper number of machines they can play at one time. It is because of this kind of misunderstanding that disputes over who was playing a machine first often occur among customers. In general, it is considered proper to play no more than two machines at one time. Both machines should be played alternately, and some coins should be allowed to remain in the tray of both machines at all times; the presence of coins in the tray should signal to other players that those machines are in use. Where exceptions to this general rule exist, signs reading "One Machine Per Customer Only" are usually placed on the front of each machine.

If you are uncertain whether someone is playing a machine that you want to try, check whether there are coins in the tray—or *ask* before you begin to play. Above all, don't barge up and accidentally play off someone's jackpot while he or she is waiting to be paid.

Reserving Your Favorite Machine

Another custom that often causes confusion is what to do if you want to continue to play the same slot machine but must visit the restroom, make a phone call, or stop for lunch or dinner. Every day, slot customers return from a short break only to find that someone else has become very comfortable playing their favorite machine. It is permissible in many casinos to request that your machine be closed while you are away. All that is necessary is to ask the floor supervisor in the slot area to reserve your machine until you return and give them a specific time when you plan to be back. If you plan to be away not more than ten or fifteen minutes, there would be no problem. If, however, you will be away longer or you would like to have lunch or dinner or take a nap, it may not be possible to close your machine for that long.

Whether the casino will reserve your machine will depend upon the length of time you request, the demand from other customers wanting to play your type of machine, and the casino's slot department policy. Do not be afraid to ask, however, to have your favorite machine held for you. Slot personnel will be happy to do it if they can.

Gratuities for Casino Personnel

Next, let's discuss gratuities, that's the polite word for *tipping*. If it's true that money talks, nowhere does it talk louder than in the gaming world, where so many people receive the majority of their income from tips. In addition to cocktail waitresses, bartenders, valet parking attendants, and the like who work for tips, there also are the keno runners and the blackjack, dice, roulette, and poker dealers (to mention only a few) whose income is principally derived from the generosity of the public. Tips are often referred to as *tokes* in the casino industry, and tokes have become such a major source of income that the IRS recently moved to make sure that casino employees in positions where toke incomes predominate are routinely and accurately reporting all such earnings.

While tokes are a way of life in the gaming business, I do not want to give the impression that unless you bend over backwards with gratitude you should expect poor service and lousy behavior from casino personnel. It is their job to earn your gratitude through providing warm, friendly, and helpful service. Do not under any circumstances reward poor performance. Never let any employee hustle or pressure you for a tip—that's rule number one.

Slot players may receive the services of several casino employees. For example, it is customary in many (but not all) casinos to offer slot customers complimentary cocktails and other beverages. Usually a cocktail waitress or slot host or hostess will offer to take your order for a cocktail, soft drink, or coffee, and will return to your machine a few minutes later with your beverage. Although there is no charge for your drinks while you are playing slots, please keep in mind that it is the beverage itself that is complimentary, not the service of the person bringing the drink. It definitely would be in order to tip this person each time you are served a drink. How much to tip is entirely up to you, of course, and should be in accord with how politely and pleasantly the individual provided this service.

As a slot player, you will probably need the services of some of the slot department personnel from time to time. In most casinos, you do not have to leave your machine when you need to buy change because you can press a button on the front of the machine to summon a change person to come to you. The change person also should be able to answer questions about your machine and in general should make you feel welcome and comfortable. If you hit a jackpot, it is likely that your change person will be one of the people who will pay you. (We are talking here about jackpots that are paid by an attendant, not jackpots paid by the machine itself.) If your change person has been courteous and helpful in previously selling you change and is deserving in your opinion, you may hand him or her a tip at the time your jackpot is paid. Again, as before, the amount of the tip is entirely up to you. A dollar or two on a jackpot of between $25 and $75–$100 would be about average.

If you have had any other transactions with slot department employees such as booth cashiers, slot mechanics, or floor people who were especially helpful and polite, you may wish to thank them with a small toke sometime while you are playing. Please remember, however, that you are not expected to tip anyone. It's an absolutely voluntary gesture that you may bestow upon the person who has earned it by making you feel like a guest instead of a customer.

I would like any slot-related casino worker who reads this to know that I've included this section on etiquette as much for them as for the slot player to whom this book is obviously intended. Casino employees have been overheard to say again and again, "Someone should tell these folks it's OK to say 'please' and 'thank you' and that tipping is not a city in China!" So, my fellow slot people, this is for you—but take notice that I have also stressed that tokes must be deserved, and only through the quality of your service can you make that happen.

As a final word on the subject, not only should mediocre service not be rewarded, poor service should be reported. If you are greeted by rude or inconsiderate employees, please bring that to the casino's attention. It's one way improvements can be made. You are the slot department's guest, and you deserve the best of treatment. Playing slots should be a leisure-time recreational activity, and the people hired to serve you should help to make your visit fun.

CHAPTER 8

A Happy Ending

As you now know, this has not been some silly book about one crazy scheme or another of how to win big on slots. There is no such thing as a successful scheme like that. Of course, you can play "smart" and greatly improve your chances of winning without throwing money away like crazy; and at least you now know how to keep from losing foolishly.

As a former manager of slots in one of the world's largest casino, I've had the pleasure on numerous occasions of paying out tens of thousands of dollars to lucky slot players. Because of these winnings, the lives of many of these people have been changed for the better, young and old alike. I remember a young woman who won a sizable jackpot and then spent a fraction of her winnings on an airline ticket so her elderly mother could fly cross-country to visit her. In the course of the visit, mother and daughter got in the car and drove for five hours so Mom could see the casino where her daughter had won. Within an hour after they arrived,

Mom hit a jackpot almost twice the size of her daughter's—on the same group of machines.

Another young woman who had the good fortune of hitting a sizable jackpot was asked how she planned to spend her winnings. She replied that the first thing she was going to do was have indoor plumbing and hot running water installed in her home! Did she need the money, or what?

Other folks, because of one lucky moment, have been able to retire early or retire very much more comfortably than they had previously planned. One such couple bought one of the most glamorous motorhomes on the market, and now they follow the sun all year long. At last report, they were in Palm Springs having a wonderful time.

Those are just some of many stories about lucky slot players that have a happy ending. Here's wishing you all the luck in the world that you may also become a very fortunate slot winner and have many happy endings.

APPENDIX

Slot Player's Win-and-Loss Diary

Date	Casino Name and Location	Machine Number	Hours Played	Coin Bought	Coin Returned	Won or <Lost>	Additional Information: Witnesses, employee names and positions, other miscellaneous details.

SLOT PLAYER'S WIN-AND-LOSS DIARY

SLOT PLAYER'S WIN-AND-LOSS DIARY

Date	Casino Name and Location	Machine Number	Hours Played	Coin Bought	Coin Returned	Won or <Lost>	Additional Information: Witnesses, employee names and positions, other miscellaneous details.

SLOT PLAYER'S WIN-AND-LOSS DIARY

Date	Casino Name and Location	Machine Number	Hours Played	Coin Bought	Coin Returned	Won or ⟨Lost⟩	Additional Information: Witnesses, employee names and positions, other miscellaneous details.

SLOT PLAYER'S WIN-AND-LOSS DIARY

Date	Casino Name and Location	Machine Number	Hours Played	Coin Bought	Coin Returned	Won or <Lost>	Additional Information: Witnesses, employee names and positions, other miscellaneous details.

SLOT PLAYER'S WIN-AND-LOSS DIARY

Date	Casino Name and Location	Machine Number	Hours Played	Coin Bought	Coin Returned	Won or \<Lost\>	Additional Information: Witnesses, employee names and positions, other miscellaneous details.

SLOT PLAYER'S WIN-AND-LOSS DIARY

Date	Casino Name and Location	Machine Number	Hours Played	Coin Bought	Coin Returned	Won or (Lost)	Additional Information: Witnesses, employee names and positions, other miscellaneous details.

SLOT PLAYER'S WIN-AND-LOSS DIARY

Date	Casino Name and Location	Machine Number	Hours Played	Coin Bought	Coin Returned	Won or <Lost>	Additional Information: Witnesses, employee names and positions, other miscellaneous details.

SLOT PLAYER'S WIN-AND-LOSS DIARY

Date	Casino Name and Location	Machine Number	Hours Played	Coin Bought	Coin Returned	Won or \<Lost\>	Additional Information: Witnesses, employee names and positions, other miscellaneous details.

SLOT PLAYER'S WIN-AND-LOSS DIARY

Date	Casino Name and Location	Machine Number	Hours Played	Coin Bought	Coin Returned	Won or <Lost>	Additional Information: Witnesses, employee names and positions, other miscellaneous details.

SLOT PLAYER'S WIN-AND-LOSS DIARY

Date	Casino Name and Location	Machine Number	Hours Played	Coin Bought	Coin Returned	Won or <Lost>	Additional Information: Witnesses, employee names and positions, other miscellaneous details.

SLOT PLAYER'S WIN-AND-LOSS DIARY

Date	Casino Name and Location	Machine Number	Hours Played	Coin Bought	Coin Returned	Won or <Lost>	Additional Information: Witnesses, employee names and positions, other miscellaneous details.

SLOT PLAYER'S WIN-AND-LOSS DIARY

Date	Casino Name and Location	Machine Number	Hours Played	Coin Bought	Coin Returned	Won or \<Lost\>	Additional Information: Witnesses, employee names and positions, other miscellaneous details.

SLOT PLAYER'S WIN-AND-LOSS DIARY

Date	Casino Name and Location	Machine Number	Hours Played	Coin Bought	Coin Returned	Won or (Lost)	Additional Information: Witnesses, employee names and positions, other miscellaneous details.

SLOT PLAYER'S WIN-AND-LOSS DIARY

Date	Casino Name and Location	Machine Number	Hours Played	Coin Bought	Coin Returned	Won or <Lost>	Additional Information: Witnesses, employee names and positions, other miscellaneous details.

SLOT PLAYER'S WIN-AND-LOSS DIARY

Date	Casino Name and Location	Machine Number	Hours Played	Coin Bought	Coin Returned	Won or (Lost)	Additional Information: Witnesses, employee names and positions, other miscellaneous details.

ABOUT THE AUTHOR

With a background as an industrial engineer and management analyst, Jim Regan came to the gaming industry in 1979 as a slots manager for one of the largest and best known casinos in the world.

He soon realized that most of the gaming public's ideas about playing slot machines were derived from superstition, myth, and a general misunderstanding about how slots actually operate. Never before did he see so many people so willing to spend so much money on something that they knew so little about.

He wrote this book, therefore, to provide all the information that slot customers would need to be able to start *playing smart.*

Prior to his gaming experience, Mr. Regan was a civilian management analyst with the U.S. Department of Defense, where he conducted transportation studies and provided related management services. He also has been a management analyst with the airline industry. In addition, he has owned and operated several personal businesses and has many years of supervisory and operational management experience.

Mr. Regan is a graduate of Arizona State University, Tempe, Arizona.

Gambling Books Ordering Information

Ask for any of the books listed below at your bookstore. Or to order direct from the publisher, call 1-800-447-BOOK (MasterCard or Visa), or send a check or money order for the books purchased (plus $4.00 shipping and handling for the first book ordered and 75¢ for each additional book) to Carol Publishing Group, 120 Enterprise Avenue, Dept. 973, Secaucus, NJ 07094.

Beating the Wheel: The System That's Won More Than $6 Million, From Las Vegas to Monte Carlo by Russell T. Barnhart
$12.95 paper   0-8184-0553-8   (CAN $15.95)

Blackjack Your Way to Riches by Richard Albert Canfield
$9.95 paper   0-8184-0498-1   (CAN $12.95)

The Body Language of Poker: Mike Caro's Book of Tells by Mike Caro
$18.95 paper   0-89746-100-2   (CAN $23.95)

Caro on Gambling by Mike Caro
$6.95 paper   0-89746-029-4   (CAN $9.95)

The Cheapskate's Guide to Las Vegas: Hotels, Gambling, Food, Entertainment, and Much More by Connie Emerson
$9.95 paper   0-8065-1530-9   (CAN $13.95)

The Complete Guide to Riverboat Gambling: It's History, and How to Play, Win and Have Fun by Scott Faragher
$12.95 paper   0-8065-1569-4   (CAN $17.95)

Darwin Ortiz on Casino Gambling: The Complete Guide to Playing and Winning by Darwin Ortiz
$12.95 paper   0-8184-0525-2   (CAN $16.95)

Gambling Scams: How They Work, How to Detect Them, How to Protect Yourself by Darwin Ortiz
$10.95 paper   0-8184-0529-5   (CAN $14.95)

Gambling Times Guide to Blackjack by Stanley Roberts
$9.95 paper   0-89746-015-4   (CAN $12.95)

Gambling Times Guide to Craps by N.B. Winkless
$9.95 paper   0-89746-013-8   (CAN $12.95)

How to be Treated Like a High Roller by Robert Renneisen
$7.95 paper   0-8184-0556-2   (CAN $9.95)

How To Win at Casino Gaming Tournaments by Haven Earle Haley
$8.95 paper   0-89746-016-2   (CAN $11.95)

John Patrick's Blackjack
$12.95 paper   0-8184-0555-4   (CAN $16.95)

John Patrick's Craps
$14.95 paper   0-8184-0554-6   (CAN $18.95)

John Patrick's Slots
$12.95 paper   0-8184-0574-0   (CAN $15.95)

The Mathematics of Gambling by Edward O. Thorp
$7.95 paper   0-89746-019-7   (CAN $10.95)

Million Dollar Blackjack by Ken Uston
$16.95 paper   0-89746-068-5   (CAN $21.95)

New Poker Games by Mike Caro
$5.95 paper   0-89746-040-5   (CAN $7.95)

Playing Blackjack as a Business by Lawrence Revere
$14.95 paper   0-8184-0064-1   (CAN $18.95)

Progression Blackjack: Exposing the Cardcounting Myth by Donald Dahl
$8.95 paper 0-8065-1396-9 (CAN $10.95)

Psyching Out Vegas: Winning Through Psychology in the Casinos of the World by Marvin Karlins, Ph.D.
$15.00 cloth   0-914314-03-3   (CAN $19.95)

Winning at Slot Machines by Jim Regan
$5.95 paper   0-8065-0973-2   (CAN $7.95)

Winning Blackjack in Atlantic City and Around the World by Thomas Gaffney
$7.95 paper   0-8065-1178-8   (CAN $10.95)

Winning Blackjack Without Counting Cards by David S. Popik
$7.95 paper   0-8065-0963-5   (CAN $10.95)

(Prices subject to change; books subject to availability)